How We Got Our Antiracist Constitution

Canonizing BROWN V. BOARD OF EDUCATION
in Courts and Minds

Jesse Merriam

Washington Fellow
The Claremont Institute's CENTER FOR THE AMERICAN WAY OF LIFE

PROVOCATIONS #6
CLAREMONT INSTITUTE
CENTER FOR THE AMERICAN WAY OF LIFE

All rights reserved. No part of this publication may be reproduced or transmitted in any form or by any means electronic or mechanical, including photocopy, recording, or any information storage and retrieval system now known or to be invented, without permission in writing from the publisher, except by a reviewer who wishes to quote brief passages in connection with a review written for inclusion in a magazine, newspaper, website, or broadcast.

Design: **David Reaboi**/Strategic Improvisation

Published in the United States by the Claremont Institute

CLAREMONT
PRESS

HOW WE GOT OUR ANTIRACIST CONSTITUTION

Canonizing BROWN V. BOARD OF EDUCATION
in Courts and Minds

In a 2019 Politico forum on how to fix American politics, one scholar's proposal stood out as particularly audacious: Ibram X. Kendi's antiracist constitutional amendment.[1] This amendment, Kendi explained, would create a new federal agency, the "Department of Anti-racism," which "would be responsible for preclearing all local, state and federal public policies to ensure they won't yield racial inequity, monitor those policies, investigate private racist policies when racial inequity surfaces, and monitor public officials for expressions of racist ideas."

Kendi's proposal scandalized conservative scholars and pundits. What about the free speech implications of monitoring private expression? And what about federalism and the separation of powers? Wouldn't the preclearing of state and local policy by a federal administrative agency dismantle the Constitution's distribution of authority?

In all their bluster, however, conservatives were missing the real scandal, which lies not in the radicalism of Kendi's proposal but in its *inefficacy*. That's right: Kendi's amendment would not fundamentally change how our legal system operates. In fact, we already have something that is arguably more powerful than an antiracist constitutional provision. We have an antiracist constitutional order that makes racial discrimination our greatest evil and racial diversity our greatest good. The product of this order is that core structural guarantees (like federalism and the state action doctrine) and fundamental individual rights (like the freedom of association, religious liberty, and freedom of speech) must be narrowed or even eliminated to the extent they interfere with these values.

The purpose of this *Provocations* essay is to explore how we came to have this antiracist constitutional order so that we can better understand how it operates.

I. HOW WE CAME TO HAVE AN ANTIRACIST CONSTITUTION

To appreciate the origins of our antiracist constitution, we first must appreciate the significance of what constitutional scholars have dubbed "canonization"[2]—that is, the process by which a single Supreme Court decision comes to control constitutional theory, debate, and interpretation.

One important effect of canonization is *institutional*. The canon instructs lawyers which values our legal system celebrates,[3] so that all our legal institutions—the courts, the legal academy, the bar—are shaped around celebrating the values represented by the canonical decision. Another important effect lies in *argument formation*. All legal arguments must be framed in such a way as to include the canonical cases,[4] so that all our methods of interpretation—whether we call the method "living constitutionalism," "originalism," or something else—follow the same basic rule: their legitimacy is framed according to whether they comport with the canon.[5] A third important effect lies in the power of *sacralization*. Canonization confers a sacred quality on a Supreme Court decision, so that its underlying values take on a quasi-religious status. The result is that any value or principle derived from that decision must prevail over any competing norms, including those expressed in the text of the Constitution itself.

Brown v. Board of Education (1954) is the paradigmatic canonical case. In fact, to say that *Brown* is in the constitutional canon is an understatement. Rather, it is more accurate to say that it is *the* canonical case, and it is perhaps even more accurate to say that *Brown* is *the canon as a whole* in that many of the other canonical cases emanate from its power. This is supported by both the empirical[6] and theoretical[7] scholarship on the constitutional canon. The canonical status of *Brown* has become such a fundamental part of our legal landscape that legal scholars have claimed there is a "*Brown* Test": No constitutional theory or interpretation is permissible within our legal system if it is inconsistent with the *Brown* decision or any of the principles and values that follow from that decision.[8]

How did *Brown* go from being part of our legal system to becoming the system itself? Unlike other forms of canonization (such as the canonization of saints in the Catholic Church), canonization of Supreme Court cases is an informal process, with no specific criteria, formal procedures, or hierarchical authority governing how it operates. Accordingly, while scholars generally agree that *Brown* is the paradigmatic canonical case, they disagree on *why* and *how* it has come to have this status. In addition to being an informal process, canonization in the judicial context is gradual, arising from decades of seeping into the sediment of constitutional culture. Canonization in constitutional law is also distinctly prescriptive. Whereas canonization in the religious context serves to recognize the preexisting order that inheres in the universe between man and God, constitutional canonization serves a normative or prescriptive purpose in ordaining what our constitutional law *should become*. As Jamal Greene has observed, *Brown* is canonical precisely because it departed from legal conventions and created a new legal order, revolving around a new set of constitutional values.

So how does this informal, gradual, transformative process operate in canonizing Supreme Court decisions? As alluded to above, there is significant scholarly disagreement on how the process works, but there seem to be three distinct phases. Understanding these phases and how they relate to the canonization of *Brown* will help us appreciate how we came to have an antiracist constitution.

The First Phase in the Canonization of *Brown*: The Construction Phase

First is what might be called "the construction phase," whereby a Supreme Court decision initiates a groundbreaking shift in constitutional law. This paradigm shift mobilizes a resistance movement, which in turn generates a series of intellectual, political, and legal battles. This conflict paves the way for the initial decision to broaden and take on a larger legal, cultural, and political significance. In this phase, the meaning of the decision is constructed through conflict.

The Supreme Court's decision in *Brown* represented the apotheosis of a revolution, the culmination of a legal strategy that began when the NAACP received a $100,000 grant from the Garland Fund.[9] Under the guidance of future Supreme Court Justice Felix Frankfurter (at that time a Harvard Law School professor and the NAACP's legal adviser), the NAACP used the Garland Fund grant to hire Nathan Margold (Frankfurter's former student and at the time the only other Jewish professor besides Frankfurter at Harvard Law School) to develop a litigation strategy for the NAACP's desegregation campaign. Following the Margold Report (as it has come to be known), the NAACP began its litigation campaign by challenging segregation in higher education, before moving to the much more controversial area of K-12 public education, culminating in the *Brown* decision.

While *Brown* completed the Margold strategy, it was unclear what the decision would mean for race relations outside the public education context. This was due to various ambiguities in the decision itself. The court, after asking the parties to submit additional briefing on whether the 39th Congress intended to create a desegregation mandate in the Fourteenth Amendment, decided to elide that historical question in its opinion. Instead, the court rested its reasoning on the fact that segregation of public schools produced "feelings of inferiority" in black children.

By focusing on this particular psychological feature of school segregation, the opinion did not resolve whether the *Plessy v. Ferguson* (1896) "separate but equal" doctrine was still good law outside the education context. Likewise, the decision did not resolve how desegregation of public education would be implemented, a task the court explicitly left for future litigation.

Although the opinion was open-ended in these ways, it was nonetheless clear in announcing two revolutionary principles. One principle was that feelings of racial inferiority have a constitutional status, thus raising the possibility that any governmental action creating such feelings, even indirectly through private actors, would be subject to close judicial scrutiny. The second principle was that racial integration is the remedy for these "feelings of inferiority."

Put together, these two principles stood for what was then a revolutionary idea: private discrimination is a constitutional evil and racial diversity is a constitutional good.

CONSTRUCTION 1:
Racial Diversity as a Constitutional Good

The *Brown* decision ushered in a new constitutional culture, an order centered around racial diversity as its chief value. As evidence of how *Brown* created this diversity culture, consider how Lisa M. Stulberg and Anthony S. Chen have found that, in the decade following the *Brown* decision, several elite universities adopted affirmative action programs as part of a new civil rights mission in higher education.[10] Similarly, in a subsequent article, Stulberg and Chen found that diversity rhetoric began with *Brown* and intensified "in 1963 as a result of rising national concern over civil rights," long before Justice Powell famously invoked diversity to justify affirmative action in his *Bakke* opinion.[11]

Brown's role in justifying affirmative action was evident in *Porcelli v. Titus*,[12] the first federal case adjudicating the legality of affirmative action preferences. The *Porcelli* case arose after the Newark School Board decided in 1968 to abandon its formal promotion procedures and use race as the principal criterion for promoting teachers to be vice-principals and principals. Ten white teachers sued the board for violating the Fourteenth Amendment and Title VII by suspending the "promotion lists" and "abolish[ing] the examination procedure for the purpose of appointing Negroes to positions for which they would not otherwise be eligible."[13]

The district court conceded that race "played a part in the Board's decision to suspend the promotion lists and abandon the examination system,"[14] but the court found that this use of race was consistent with the Fourteenth Amendment and Title VII because "the Board had the authority to take such steps as it deemed necessary and proper to promote the educational welfare of the Newark school community."[15] The Third Circuit affirmed the decision and even suggested that Newark's racial preferences were not only permitted but *required* under the Fourteenth Amendment. According to the Third Circuit, because using the formal promotion procedures would have the effect of advantaging whites over blacks, this color-blind approach "would be in negation of the Fourteenth Amendment to the Constitution and the line of cases which have followed *Brown v. Board of Education*."[16] In other words, by making integration the remedy for "feelings of inferiority," *Brown* made diversity a constitutional good, so that affirmative action was not only permitted but even required under the Fourteenth Amendment.

CONSTRUCTION 2:
Private Discrimination as a Constitutional Evil

By making racial diversity a constitutional good, the *Brown* revolution also made private discrimination that works against racial diversity a constitutional evil. This is not only evident in the various anti-discrimination mandates featured in the post-*Brown* civil rights legislation but also in how courts rejected the "freedom of choice" plans that school boards adopted as a remedy for *Brown*. These "freedom of choice" plans gave parents the right to choose which neighborhood schools their children attended. The result of these plans was that public schools remained almost exclusively white or black, because white and black parents alike generally preferred for their children to attend schools with members of their own racial group.

At first, the federal courts tentatively accepted these "freedom of choice" plans as satisfying the *Brown* decision,[17] but this changed after the Department of Health, Education, and Welfare (HEW) issued desegregation guidelines for satisfying the Civil Rights Act of 1964. Under these HEW guidelines, issued in 1965 and 1966, "freedom of choice" plans were permissible only if there was actual evidence of integration accompanying the choice. In other words, choice was permissible only if it involved the *right* choice—the pro-diversity choice.

Three Fifth Circuit opinions—all written by Judge John Minor Wisdom between 1965 and 1966—followed these HEW guidelines by asserting that *Brown* required positive governmental action to encourage integration and therefore stood opposed to programs that facilitated freedom of association.[18] As Judge Wisdom explained in the *Jefferson* case, the *Brown* decision means that the Constitution is both color-blind and color-conscious because, in Judge Wisdom's view, the Equal Protection Clause was designed to eliminate both private and public racial discrimination: "The Constitution is both color blind and color conscious. To avoid conflict with the equal protection clause, a [governmental] classification that denies a benefit, causes harm, or imposes a burden must not be based on race. In that sense the Constitution is color blind. But the Constitution is color conscious to prevent discrimination being perpetuated and to undo the effects of past discrimination."

In 1967, the Fifth Circuit decided to rehear one of these Judge Wisdom opinions on an *en banc* basis (*en banc* means that the entire circuit sits together as a panel to decide the case). In that case, known as *Jefferson II*, the Fifth Circuit adopted Justice Wisdom's understanding of *Brown* as forbidding "freedom of choice" plans.[19] In the Fifth Circuit's view, "Freedom of choice is not a goal in itself. It is a means to an end." Again, private choice was held to be permissible under *Brown* only if it produced the right choice—the pro-diversity choice.

The following year, in *Green v. County School Board* (1968), the US Supreme Court confirmed Judge Wisdom's understanding by holding that "freedom of choice" plans are unconstitutional under *Brown*. In the court's view, the *Brown* decision required school boards "to take whatever steps might be necessary to convert to [an integrated] system in which racial discrimination would be eliminated root and branch." Because "freedom of choice" plans facilitated the private expression of racial discrimination, these plans were unconstitutional. Moreover, the court added, anything short of producing immediate diversity was impermissible: "The burden on a school board today is to come forward with a plan that promises realistically to work, and promises realistically to work *now*."

In sum, by the close of the 1960s, *Brown* had been constructed to generate two revolutionary principles: (1) racial diversity is a constitutional good, and (2) private racial discrimination is a constitutional evil. But at this point these were not yet sacred principles in our constitutional system. For that to happen, *Brown* itself had to be canonized. And that would require two more steps.

The Second Phase in the Canonization of *Brown*: The Submission Phase

The next critical step in canonizing a Supreme Court decision is "the submission phase," whereby critics of the initial decision capitulate to the new paradigm. Through submission, the canonical case, as well as all the judicial decisions and statutes associated with it, become entrenched in the legal system. Whereas the construction phase has a *broadening* effect, enlarging the scope of the canonical case to encompass new principles, the submission phase has a *deepening* effect, so that those principles can seep into the bedrock of law.

To appreciate the extent of the submission to *Brown*, it is first important to get a sense of what preceded submission—that is, the resistance against *Brown*. There was, of course, a vigorous backlash against *Brown* throughout the South, represented most poignantly by protests at schoolhouse doors and the 1956 Declaration of Constitutional Principles (known as the "Southern Manifesto") signed by nineteen US senators and eighty-two representatives. But there was also significant criticism among Northern intellectual and political elites. This Northern resistance would prove much more important in terms of canonizing the *Brown* decision, because the eventual Northern submission played a critical role in solidifying the nation's institutions behind the principles that diversity is a constitutional good and discrimination is a constitutional evil.

The Pre-Submission Resistance Against *Brown*

The most important expression of the intellectual resistance against *Brown* outside the South was in the commentary at the recently formed *National Review*, the publication most responsible for structuring the conservative movement that would soon become merged with the Republican Party.[20] Between 1955 (when *National Review* was formed) and 1968 (which roughly marks the end of the *Brown* construction phase), *National Review* published more than thirty-five articles on the *Brown* decision. Of all these articles, I was unable to find a single one that did not treat the decision negatively. Many of these 1955-1968 *National Review* criticisms of *Brown* were featured in major articles, including several by leading *National Review* writers and conservative intellectuals, such as Frank Meyer,[21] James Burnham,[22] Willmoore Kendall,[23] and Richard Weaver.[24] William F. Buckley wrote a few such articles himself.[25] During this period, there were also many editorial articles on *Brown*.[26]

These conservative anti-*Brown* arguments were assembled in a more comprehensive matter in 1966, when L. Brent Bozell II (Buckley's brother-in-law and cofounder of *National Review*) published *The Warren Revolution* (1966), a nearly four hundred-page polemic against what the Warren Court was doing to constitutional law. The first chapter of the book was devoted to how *Brown* represented a revolution against the American constitutional order, principally because it was inconsistent with the purpose and text of the Fourteenth Amendment.

There were also prominent attacks on the *Brown* decision from figures not clearly associated with the conservative movement or right-wing thought. In fact, two such attacks came from two of the most distinguished legal authorities in the country. In 1958, Judge Learned Hand, a Second Circuit judge and the most influential judge never to be appointed to the Supreme Court, discussed *Brown* as part of his Oliver Wendell Holmes Lectures at Harvard Law School. In his Holmes Lectures, Judge Hand explained that *Brown* represented an illegitimate exercise of judicial authority.[27] The following year's Holmes Lectures were even more controversial. These lectures were given by Herbert Wechsler, arguably the most prominent scholar in the country at the time.[28] Just as Judge Hand had done, Wechsler used his Holmes Lectures to criticize the *Brown* decision, but Wechsler went even further than Hand by making *Brown* the focus of his presentation. Wechsler criticized the *Brown* decision on the ground that the decision did not rest on a neutral principle and therefore failed to satisfy a basic requirement of the rule of law. Wechsler explained how, despite his personal views (like Judge Hand, Wechsler was a New Deal liberal who favored racial integration), he could not find a neutral basis for extending the freedom of association to parents who preferred to send their children to racially diverse schools while denying the freedom of association to parents who preferred to send their children to racially homogeneous schools. Wechsler later turned these lectures into a *Harvard Law Review* article, "Toward Neutral Principles of Constitutional Law," which became the fifth most cited law review article in American history.

There were significant intellectual critiques outside the legal world as well. For example, in a 1955 letter to the

Orlando Sentinel, Zora Neale Hurston, one of the leading black writers in the country, explained how she found the *Brown* decision "as insulting rather than honoring [her] race." What she found particularly insulting was the "diversity rationale" mentioned above—that is, the idea that integration is a constitutional good in itself because of the association it brings between the races. As she put it, "Since the days of the never-to-be-sufficiently deplored Reconstruction, there has been current the belief that there is no great[er] delight to Negroes than physical association with whites." Hurston further explained how she worried that the *Brown* ruling was merely the first step in a revolution that would "do away with the two-party system and arrive at Govt by administrative decree," so that "Govt by fiat [would] replace the Constitution."

Similarly, in 1959, Hannah Arendt, at the time one of the nation's most distinguished political theorists, published in *Dissent Magazine* an article titled "Reflections on Little Rock," which criticized *Brown* and suggested that the decision could serve as a catalyst for a totalitarian movement organized around the elimination of private interpersonal discrimination.[29] Like Hurston, Arendt focused on how the logic of *Brown* drew no distinctions between the public and private spheres, thus raising the possibility that the federal government could use the *Brown* decision as the basis for monitoring and regulating all interpersonal interactions, so that *Brown* would become a source of rather than a limitation on governmental authority.[30]

Submission Begins: The Nixon Administration and the Rehnquist Confirmation Hearing

The liberal critics of *Brown* were the first to capitulate to the new constitutional order. For example, after her article was met with furious criticism from her liberal colleagues, Arendt explained that, as a European, she did not fully understand American race relations, and moreover, as a Jew, she sympathized with the black American cause. Arendt declined to pursue the argument in later writings.

By the 1960s, it was nearly unimaginable that a liberal scholar would criticize the *Brown* decision. As Ken Kersch notes, Herbert Wechsler and the other Legal Process scholars shifted their positions on judicial power and individual rights in order to comply with the liberal position on *Brown*.[31] It is not an overstatement to say that *Brown* effectively killed Wechsler's Legal Process School, a significant feat, given that, before *Brown*, the Legal Process School represented a leading view of judicial power within the legal academy.

Conservatives gradually but ineluctably followed their liberal counterparts. In his 1968 presidential campaign, Richard Nixon sought to carve out a middle-road position on *Brown* and civil rights—a position between the anti–civil rights position held by the third-party candidate (Alabama governor George Wallace) and the pro–civil rights position held by the Democratic candidate (Hubert Humphrey, the lead author of the 1964 Civil Rights Act). Nixon thus "campaigned on a platform supporting freedom of choice"[32] and "strict construction" of the Constitution (to peel off some of the Southern support for Wallace) while avoiding direct criticism of the *Brown* opinion (to retain moderate Republican voters in the North). This strategy worked, with Wallace winning only a handful of states (all in the Deep South).

Once elected, however, Nixon pivoted toward the center by distancing himself from any criticism of *Brown*. In 1969, Nixon adopted what came to be known as "the Philadelphia Plan," an even more aggressive federal affirmative action program than the ones adopted by the Kennedy and Johnson administrations. Nixon's shift on civil rights was solidified on March 24, 1970, when he gave a speech on race and education policy. The speech was a response to criticism of Nixon for nominating Judge Harrold Carswell to replace Justice Abe Fortas on the US Supreme Court. Carswell was a Southerner who had openly criticized *Brown* and the civil rights movement. As it became apparent that the Senate would reject Judge Carswell's nomination because of his statements on *Brown*, Nixon sought to distance himself from Carswell by giving a speech pledging his own commitment to *Brown*. As Nixon pronounced, his "specific objective" in giving the speech was "to reaffirm [his] personal belief that the 1954 decision of the Supreme Court in *Brown v. Board of Education* was right in both constitutional and human terms."

Professor Brad Snyder, in his article on how conservatives canonized *Brown*, identifies this speech as the turning point in conservative treatment of the decision, paving the way for the Rehnquist confirmation hearing in 1971. Rehnquist's confirmation hearing focused extensively on his views on the *Brown* decision, owing in part to Rehnquist's outspoken hostility toward civil rights as a private lawyer in Arizona. When asked in his 1971 confirmation hearing about *Brown*, Rehnquist refused to express his personal views on the decision, but he consistently recited how *Brown* was settled law because it was decided unanimously and had been affirmed in subsequent cases.

After Rehnquist's nomination moved to floor debates, the controversy over *Brown* intensified as a result of *Newsweek* magazine publishing a 1952 memo that Rehnquist had written as Justice Jackson's clerk in support of upholding *Plessy v. Ferguson* (1896). *Newsweek*'s publication of the 1952 memo, Brad Snyder writes, "made it starkly clear to Rehnquist that embracing *Brown*'s validity was the only way to salvage his nomination."

To avoid Judge Carswell's fate, Rehnquist took the extraordinary measure of writing a letter to Senator Eastland (chairman of the Senate Judiciary Committee). In that letter, Rehnquist explained how he had not been afforded an opportunity in his confirmation hearing to pledge his personal commitment to *Brown*, because the hearing focused on the legal status of the decision, not Rehnquist's own views on the subject. To clarify any ambiguity left in his confirmation hearing, Rehnquist pledged his personal fidelity to *Brown*, ending the letter with the following proclamation: "I wish to state unequivocally that I fully support the legal reasoning and the rightness from the standpoint of fundamental fairness of the *Brown* decision."

The Senate rewarded Rehnquist's recitation of the *Brown* oath with confirmation to the Supreme Court, thereby signaling that *Brown* was taking on a distinct role in our political and legal culture. To participate in public discourse, a person had to go beyond merely accepting the decision as settled law—indeed, there was now pressure to embrace the decision as a personal matter.

The effect on conservative discourse was immediate, as reflected in the commentary at *National Review*. In 1973, *National Review* featured two non-negative treatments of the *Brown* decision, with each article criticizing the decision but finding something good to say about it. Notably, these two articles were written, respectively, by William F. Buckley and James Kilpatrick—two men who, just a decade earlier, had been the publication's fiercest critics of *Brown*.[33] In August 1976, Jack Chatfield—a civil rights activist, a Trinity College professor, and a close friend of George Will—wrote the first pro-*Brown* article for *National Review*.[34]

Submission Accelerates: The Second Rehnquist Confirmation and the Bork Debacle

Submission to *Brown* accelerated in the 1980s, principally as a result of pressure applied by Democratic senators in Supreme Court confirmation hearings. In 1986, when Associate Justice Rehnquist was nominated to be chief justice, his confirmation hearings again focused on his position on *Brown*. But once again, he professed his fidelity to *Brown*. And this time he had the opportunity to explain that his 1952 memo was written to reflect Justice Jackson's position rather than his own personal views.

Just as had been the case in 1971, a controversy arose in the floor debates over Rehnquist's views on *Brown*, this time over the constitutional amendment Rehnquist had drafted while serving as Nixon's assistant attorney general (Nixon considered in 1970 a potential constitutional amendment that would undermine enforcement of *Brown*). But by this point, Rehnquist had accumulated enough trust through his fifteen-year tenure as associate justice that he was confirmed relatively easily to be chief justice, without having to write another letter pledging his oath to *Brown*.

One year later, however, Robert Bork was not so lucky. As a Yale law professor and DC circuit judge, Robert Bork had been an outspoken defender of orthodox originalism. Although he had never explicitly challenged *Brown*, he was a vociferous critic of the Warren Court's expansive interpretation of the Fourteenth Amendment, which raised questions about the centerpiece of that legacy—*Brown* and related civil rights cases. In addition, Bork had written a 1963 *New Republic* essay opposing the civil rights bill.[35] Even though Bork did end up defending *Brown* in his 1987 confirmation hearing, many senators and legal scholars found his commitment to *Brown* and civil rights wanting, resulting in the Senate's refusal to confirm him.[36]

With the rejection of Bork, a new rule governing the federal judiciary emerged: If a judge endorsed a particular method of interpreting the Constitution, that method had to yield *Brown* as the right decision.[37]

Legal conservatives thus had a serious dilemma on their hands. At the time of the Bork confirmation, legal conservatism was ascendant. Attorney General Meese had just announced in 1985 that the Department of Justice was committed to originalism as the correct way of doing constitutional law. In 1986, President Reagan had appointed Antonin Scalia, the first open originalist to serve on the Supreme Court. And the Federalist Society, which had been created in Reagan's first term, was starting to coalesce around originalism as a theory of law that could unite the disparate factions of the conservative movement. Bork's failed confirmation signaled that if conservatives wanted to continue their ascendancy within the legal academy and the federal judiciary, they would have to modify how originalism operated. They would have to transform originalism into a more flexible form of interpretation so that *Brown* could at least be plausibly defended as a matter of originalist theory. Once this happened, the final stage of canonization entered the picture: the weaponization phase.

The Final Phase in the Canonization of *Brown*:
The Weaponization Phase

The final stage of canonization is "the weaponization phase," which begins when the former critics marshal the decision and its values for their own legal and political agenda. As the decision becomes part and parcel of the arsenal of the former critics, the decision enters a canonical status. At this point, the case takes on a "jurisgenerative" or lawmaking role, producing legal principles far outside its original context and defeating any legal norms that stand in the way of these principles. The greater the law-making power of the canonical case, the closer to the core of the canon the case becomes.

Once again, *National Review* provides a helpful guide in marking the trajectory of conservative thought on *Brown* and its progeny. In the nearly forty years since the Bork confirmation hearing, *National Review* has published over seventy-five articles on the *Brown* decision, and of these articles, I could find only five that have treated the decision negatively (two of these five negative articles, incidentally, were written by Thomas Sowell)[38]; and I could find only twelve that were mixed in their treatment (criticizing some feature of *Brown* while not criticizing the overall result). The rest, constituting most of the articles, have been positive.

This trend, of course, shows the extent of conservative submission to *Brown*, but even more startling is that over the years this treatment has transitioned in tone from positive to reverential, to the point that conservatives have imbued *Brown* with a moral significance that separates it from all other Supreme Court decisions. This reverence for *Brown* was fully on display in 2004, when *National Review* celebrated *Brown*'s fiftieth anniversary, with several articles exploring how the decision represents the American ideal.[39] Over the last twenty years, many *National Review* writers haven even invoked a religious tone in discussing *Brown*—claiming that the decision speaks "eternal truths,"[40] is a "hallowed decision,"[41] and "definitively established a magnificent new public morality that racism is wrong."[42]

As conservatives sacralized the decision, they also began to appropriate it for their own agenda. A critical point in this development arose in 1995, when Michael McConnell, at the time a professor at University of Chicago Law School, wrote the first sustained defense of *Brown* as an originalist matter (principally on the ground that the anti-discrimination views expressed by the

Radical Republicans, in debating the 1875 Civil Rights Act, could be considered part of the original public meaning of the Fourteenth Amendment, which had been ratified seven years earlier).[43] McConnell's "originalist" defense of *Brown* was a watershed moment, because it meant not only that conservatives could now defend *Brown* as an originalist decision,[44] but also that conservatives could treat civil rights as a conservative position.[45]

By sacralizing and appropriating *Brown*, conservatives were now able to marshal it for their own purposes. Again, *National Review*'s trajectory provides significant insight into this process. In my research I was not able to find, in the twenty-two years between the creation of *National Review* and the Bork confirmation hearing, a single article using or discussing the *Brown* decision outside its original context of race and civil rights. I was able to find a few such uses between 1988 and 2000. But after 2000, the majority of the discussions of *Brown* were featured in articles that used *Brown* as a weapon in areas of law far removed from race and civil rights.[46]

This weaponizing of *Brown* has made its way into litigation strategy and legal argumentation. In *Voucher Wars* (2003), Clint Bolick (founder of the Institute for Justice) recounts his legal strategy in defending voucher programs, including the culmination of this strategy in the US Supreme Court. At one point in the book, Bolick recounts how, in litigating the Milwaukee voucher program, he used various media channels to portray the pro-voucher position as fulfilling the promise of *Brown* so that voucher opponents would be seen as "opposing a program whose primary beneficiaries were black schoolchildren." By using this strategy, Bolick sought to "savage" anyone who opposed vouchers "as a modern-day Orval Faubus, blocking the schoolhouse doors to minority schoolchildren." This logic ended up playing a central role in Bolick's argument in the Wisconsin Supreme Court, where he rested his defense of the Milwaukee voucher program on "the sacred constitutional promise of equal educational opportunities, articulated in *Brown v. Board of Education.*" Likewise, when the Cleveland voucher program came before the US Supreme Court in *Zelman v. Simmons-Harris* (2002), on whether the Cleveland program violated the Establishment Clause by using tax dollars to fund religious institutions, Bolick explicitly invoked *Brown* as a basis for why the program was constitutional.[47] The weaponization of *Brown* meant that voucher advocates could derive legal power from the moral authority of the civil rights movement.

With this conservative weaponization of *Brown*, the canonization process was now complete. The result is the political world we inhabit today, where every public official—whether Republican or Democrat, conservative or liberal, originalist or living constitutionalist—must adhere to the belief that *Brown* constitutes the moral core of our constitutional order. In this political system, all the players are rewarded and penalized according to the moral values derived from the canonization of *Brown*.

Between the conclusion of the civil rights movement in the late 1960s and the canonization of *Brown* in the mid-1990s, taking an oath to *Brown*, the way that Nixon and Rehnquist were forced to do, was sufficient. But in our post-canonization political world, *Brown* requires much more. Now our leaders must take an oath not just to *Brown* as a legal decision but to antiracism (including the notions that diversity is a constitutional good and discrimination is a constitutional evil) as a political ideology and moral commitment.

This was recently on display in Amy Coney Barrett's 2020 Supreme Court confirmation hearing, where she went out of her way to personalize her commitments not just to *Brown* but to racial equity as a public morality and political movement. She explained how, as a mother of two adopted black children, she found George Floyd's death "very, very personal"—so personal that, on the day of Floyd's death, she "wept" with her black daughter over the "kind of brutality" that "would be a risk to her [black] brother or [future] son."

Before the canonization of *Brown*, such a personal diversion about weeping with one's child would be seen as bizarre in a confirmation hearing focused on judicial temperament and legal acumen. If anything, it would demonstrate incompetence for the nominee to infer that the son or grandson of an eminent federal judge is at "risk" of suffering such "brutality" in a nation of 330 million that has roughly fifteen unarmed black men dying at the hands of police officers each year.[48]

But in a system governed by *Brown*, Barrett's statement was perfectly sensible—and her statement was in fact applauded by the conservative and liberal media alike—because showcasing one's personal (and, better yet, familial) commitment to racial diversity and equity, even in an illogical and statistically illiterate way, demonstrates that one is "acculturated," to use Balkin's and Levinson's phrasing, to our system that makes racial diversity its greatest good and racial discrimination its greatest evil. This is what our antiracist constitutional order requires.

II. HOW THE ANTIRACIST CONSTITUTION WORKS

Now that we have established how the canonization of *Brown* has produced a system in which all political and legal actors are "acculturated" to the propositions that racial discrimination is our greatest constitutional evil and racial diversity is our greatest constitutional good, we can examine how this system works in practice. As I will explain below, there are two classes of constitutional guarantees that have been narrowed as a result of the canonization of *Brown*.

The Narrowing of Structural Guarantees

The most significant structural guarantee in our Constitution is federalism—the notion that the states have an authority that is independent of the federal government. The division of federal and state authority was the single most important issue in the 1787 Constitutional Convention, and it appears throughout the Constitution—most notably in the carefully enumerated powers extended to Congress in Article I, Section 8; the limited jurisdiction given to the federal judiciary in Article III; and the explicit preservation of state sovereignty in the Tenth Amendment.

The civil rights revolution, however, just about eliminated federalism from our constitutional order. During this period, the Supreme Court expanded the federal judiciary's authority through the so-called "incorporation doctrine," subjecting the state and local governments to the first eight constitutional amendments (which were originally designed to limit only the federal government). Likewise, when several states disagreed with the validity of the *Brown* decision, the Supreme Court expanded its power of judicial review by asserting its authority as the ultimate voice on constitutional matters.

During this period, Congress also expanded its authority for the purpose of eliminating racial discrimination. For example, Congress used the Commerce Clause as its basis for passing both Title II of the Civil Rights Act of 1964 (prohibiting discrimination by public accommodations like restaurants) and Title VII of the Act (prohibiting employment discrimination). Likewise, Congress used the Taxing and Spending Clause as its basis for Title VI, which prohibits discrimination by private institutions that receive federal funding. The Civil Rights Act represented the first time that Congress sought to regulate private interpersonal social relations under these two constitutional provisions.

Nevertheless, the Supreme Court upheld the constitutionality of the Civil Rights Act, and in the course of doing so, the Supreme Court rejected Tenth Amendment arguments against the federal judiciary's and Congress's intervention in local affairs. As a result, the Tenth Amendment has essentially been read out of the Constitution, so that it now has no force under Supreme Court case law.

Another structural guarantee to fall by the wayside is the state action doctrine. The state action doctrine holds that constitutional limitations generally apply only to governmental actors, not to private conduct. Indeed, in the original Constitution, as well as in the first ten Amendments (what we now call the Bill of Rights), there was not a single limitation placed on private conduct. The first—and at this point the only—constitutional limitation on private actors appeared in the Thirteenth Amendment, banning involuntary servitude. But outside that narrow exception, the Constitution applies only to the government's actions.

The state action doctrine is, as the court explained in *Lugar v. Edmonson Oil* (1982), "a fundamental [feature] of our political order." This is for two related reasons. One, the state action doctrine preserves a distinct sphere of autonomy for private actors and associations by restricting the Constitution's limitations to governmental actors. Two, it confines the scope of judicial review and federal power by constraining the federal judiciary's oversight of private interpersonal affairs.

In the 150 years between the Founding and the beginning of the civil rights movement, the state action doctrine stood firm and the Constitution limited only governmental actors. But in the 1940s, the Supreme

Court began carving out exceptions to the doctrine, often times for explicitly racial reasons. For example, in *Smith v. Allwright* (1944), the Supreme Court held that the Texas Democratic Party violated the Equal Protection Clause by limiting its primary election to white voters, because even though a political party is a private association, the court held that the Texas Democratic Party performed a governmental function in organizing its primary election. A few years later, in *Shelley v. Kramer* (1948), the Supreme Court ruled that racially restrictive covenants (contracts restricting the sale of real property on the basis of the buyer's race) are unconstitutional, because even though they are private agreements, the enforcement of the agreement would require judicial action. Likewise, in *Burton v. Wilmington Parking Authority* (1961), the Supreme Court held that a private restaurant's refusal to serve blacks violated the Equal Protection Clause, because the restaurant rented its space from the Parking Authority of Wilmington, Delaware, and this created a sufficient nexus between the government and the restaurant to make the restaurant's discrimination state action. Similarly, in *Reitman v. Mulkey* (1967), the Supreme Court held that a private landlord's racial discrimination violated the Equal Protection Clause, because California had recently amended its state constitution to permit housing discrimination, and this amendment, according to the court, provided an incentive for landlords to discriminate, so that the resulting discrimination became state action. Several years later, the court extended this principle in *Norwood v. Harrison* (1973), holding that a private school's exclusion of black students violated the Equal Protection Clause, because the school participated in a Mississippi program providing free textbooks to private schools, and the use of these textbooks in the school's curriculum therefore made the school's discrimination state action.

Homeowners, restaurants, landlords, private schools—these are paradigmatic private actors. Before the civil rights revolution, it would have been unfathomable to consider them state actors. But after the revolution, these private agents magically became state actors, subject to the federal judiciary's oversight, when they discriminated on the basis of race.

This is the inverted scheme wrought by the antiracist constitutional order. In the old order, natural rights constituted the touchstone of the system, so the state action doctrine had a significant role in limiting the Constitution to government actors and carving out spaces for private choices and associations. But in the new order created by the civil rights revolution, eradicating discrimination and promoting diversity displaced natural rights as the system's ultimate values. In this new system, the state action doctrine no longer protects private conduct from government regulation. Instead, interpersonal relations must be subject to constant government oversight and management to eradicate discrimination.

The Narrowing of Individual Rights

Aside from structural guarantees, individual rights have also been narrowed under the antiracist constitution. This is perhaps most evident in the trajectory of the freedom of association.

The freedom of association is not explicitly mentioned in the Constitution, but it constitutes the core liberty in the Founders' conception of natural rights. Accordingly, before the civil rights revolution made private racial discrimination a constitutional evil, federal and state courts regularly upheld the freedom of association as a central feature of liberty. Indeed, in a 1924 case, the Supreme Court provided a long list of citations for how "it is the right, 'long recognized,' of a trader engaged in an entirely private business, 'freely to exercise his own independent discretion as to the parties with whom he will deal.'"[49] Even on the precipice of the civil rights revolution, courts continued to hold that "absent conspiracy or monopolization, a seller engaged in a private business may normally refuse to deal with a buyer for any reason or with no reason whatever." [50]

This freedom, however, steadily narrowed as the civil rights revolution subsumed more and more of our legal system. This began when *Shelley* eliminated the freedom of association as applied to private property agreements, and it expanded when *Brown* and its progeny limited the freedom of association in the realm of public education by forbidding "freedom of choice" school plans. But the real firepower came from two statutes: the Civil Rights Act of 1964 (which limited the freedom of association as applied to public accommodations, private employers, and private institutions receiving federal funding) and the Fair Housing Act of 1968 (which extended this limitation to real estate transactions).

In the face of these statutes, the court's freedom of association jurisprudence had to narrow even further. Accordingly, in *Newman v. Piggie Park Enterprises, Inc.* (1968), the Supreme Court rejected a constitutional claim by Maurice Bessinger (the owner of several barbeque restaurants and the Baptist head of the National Association for the Preservation of White People) that he had a freedom of association right to violate the Civil Rights Act by excluding blacks from his businesses. Likewise, in *Runyon v. McCrary* (1976), the Supreme Court held that a private school did not have a freedom of association right to discriminate on the basis of race.

What had been a long-recognized and fundamental right in the American order is now a nearly nonexistent right. And that is because antiracism has consumed our constitutional system, so that anti-discrimination is our ultimate good, making associational liberties unpalatable to our sensibilities. For this reason, modern-day freedom of association claims must be pursued through other constitutional vehicles, producing strained and often times disingenuous arguments.

To see how this works in practice, consider the constitutional reasoning employed in two recent Supreme Court cases involving disputes between conservative Christians and gay rights advocates: *Masterpiece Cakeshop v. Colorado Civil Rights Commission* (2018) and *Fulton v. City of Philadelphia* (2021).

Antiracist Constitutional Reasoning in Practice

Masterpiece Cakeshop v. Colorado Civil Rights Commission (2018) involved a dispute over whether Colorado's anti-discrimination law could lawfully punish Jack Phillips, a Christian baker, for refusing to perform particular bakery services for a same-sex wedding. Before the civil rights revolution, this would have been an easy case: Jack Phillips could simply invoke the Supreme Court's freedom of association doctrine, holding that a private business owner has the "long recognized" right "to exercise his own independent discretion as to the parties with whom he will deal." But in our post-canonization legal world, Jack Phillips did not have a strong case against the Colorado law, for the freedom of association was no longer available as a constitutional argument. In fact, none of the briefs relied on the freedom of association, because, as explained above, it has essentially been wiped from our constitutional order owing to the canonization of *Brown*. Instead, Jack Phillips had to make a religious liberty argument (on the ground that Colorado was targeting Christianity with its enforcement of anti-discrimination law) and free speech argument (on the ground that Colorado was coercing his artistic expression by penalizing him for not baking the wedding cake). Neither of these arguments is compelling, but they were the only available options after the freedom of association was no longer on the table.

Nevertheless, even though Jack Phillips's lawyers sought to avoid the specter of racial discrimination by framing this as a dispute over religious liberty and free speech, the topic of race was just as pervasive in the oral argument as the actual topics at issue.[51]

Why did race play such a significant role in the oral argument? Because both positions—the liberal position favoring Colorado and the conservative position favoring Jack Phillips—were operating within our antiracist constitutional order. Indeed, here is how David Cole, the National Legal Director of the ACLU, began his argument on behalf of the gay couple:

> Mr. Chief Justice, and may it please the Court: We don't doubt the sincerity of Mr. Phillips's convictions. But to accept his argument leads to unacceptable consequences. A bakery could refuse to sell a birthday cake to a black family if it objected to celebrating black lives.

This is how the antiracist constitutional order works. Here, at the very start of his argument, David Cole was conceding that it does not matter what Jack Phillips believes. Nor does it matter that religious liberty is specifically guaranteed in the First Amendment. All that matters is that protecting Jack Phillips's religious liberty could conceivably increase the amount of racial discrimination in society. And that is an "unacceptable consequence." In other words, in our antiracist constitutional order, legal texts have been subordinated to antiracist values, and reality has been subordinated to possibility, so that the hypothetical possibility of an event not protected by the Constitution has greater constitutional power than an actual event explicitly protected by the Constitution.

The opposing side—represented by Kristen Waggoner for the Alliance Defending Freedom and Solicitor General Noel Francisco for the Trump administration—was just as willing to operate within this paradigm, according to which racial discrimination is our greatest evil. For example, when Justice Kagan asked Waggoner if it would be the "same case or not the same case, if your client instead objected to an interracial marriage?" Waggoner answered, "Very different case in that context." After Waggoner failed to provide a reason to support this distinction, Justice Kagan probed her with the following question: "You're just saying race is different?" Waggoner had a simple response: "Yes." In our antiracist constitutional order, reasons for excepting racial discrimination from constitutional protection are not required.

This was also the Trump administration's position in defending Jack Phillips on free speech grounds. Indeed, in asserting that Jack Phillips had a free speech right not to make an expressive display for a wedding he objected to, Solicitor General Francisco said that this would *not* apply to free speech relating to race. Just as Justice Kagan probed Waggoner in the religious liberty context, Justice Ginsburg asked the solicitor general the same question applied to free speech: "So you . . . might put race in a different category, right?" The solicitor general answered: "I think race is particularly unique." After Justice Ginsburg probed whether the Trump administration's position on free speech would extend to discrimination on the basis of gender, national origin, and religion, the solicitor general said the Free Speech Clause would protect everything—except racial discrimination: "I think pretty much everything but race would fall in the same category."

This is an extraordinary statement. The United States was willing to make a bold defense of free speech as protecting discrimination against all sorts of groups—gays, women, Italians, Jews, Muslims, the elderly, the disabled, you name it. But even in this bold defense, the United States stopped at race.

Perhaps even more extraordinary is that the *Masterpiece* case was probably the most controversial and divisive Supreme Court decision of 2018. And it featured lawyers fundamentally at odds with one another. Indeed, the ACLU has treated ADF as a "hate group";[52] and it systematically waged "lawfare" against the Trump administration at every turn.[53] And yet, in the *Masterpiece* oral argument, the ACLU, the ADF, the State of Colorado, and the Trump administration could agree on one thing: A norm that does not appear explicitly in our Constitution governs how we must interpret the document, to the extent that this norm can even prevail over what is textually guaranteed in the document. In other words, they all adhere to the antiracist constitution.

The *Fulton* case was billed as *Masterpiece* Part II, in that it involved another battle between religious liberty and gay rights (the case involved Philadelphia's refusal to contract with Catholic Social Services for foster care because of CSS's unwillingness to certify same-sex couples as foster parents). Just like in *Masterpiece*, the oral argument was revealing of a court fundamentally motivated by race.[54] Justice Barrett was particularly interested in this issue, asking the CSS counsel, Lori Windham, senior counsel at the Becket Fund for Religious Liberty, the following question: "What if there was an agency who believed that interracial marriage was an offense against God and, therefore, objected to certifying interracial couples as foster families?" This question invited Windham to assert that that the "government has a compelling interest in eradicating racial discrimination"—meaning that constitutional guarantees like religious liberty and free speech can be defeated by our commitment to antiracism.

A similar conversation occurred between Justice Breyer and the Trump administration (which sided with CSS).

Justice Breyer asked Hashim M. Moopan (at the time, counselor to the solicitor general) about discrimination based on various characteristics, and Moopan answered: "I would differentiate the interracial marriage from the rest of them, Your Honor. I—on interracial marriage, this Court has made clear repeatedly that there's a particularly compelling interest in eradicating racial discrimination." Justice Breyer then asked for clarification of both the Becket Fund's and Trump administration's positions: "I want to interrupt you right here because now two of you have said this, that we should write an opinion which says discrimination on the basis of race, constitutionally speaking, is different than discrimination on the basis of gender, on the basis of religion, on the basis of nationality, on the basis of homosexuality, all right? Is that the opinion you want us to write?" Moopan then answered that this is what American constitutional law required because "eradicating that type of racial discrimination pretends—presents a particularly unique and compelling interest."

Just as she did in the *Masterpiece* case, Justice Kagan searched for the rationality underlying this distinction: "You said that the City of Philadelphia could not do the same thing with respect to race... I'm seeking to find out a reason why." Moopan answered, "The—the reason why is because—because racial discrimination is particularly unique and compelling." Frustrated with this circular reasoning (that is, the argument that racial discrimination is different from sexual orientation discrimination because racial discrimination is "particularly unique"), Justice Kagan cut Moopan off and asked facetiously whether he was saying that the government's interest in eradicating racial discrimination is "super-compelling." Moopan agreed that Kagan's facetious representation was his actual argument: "That's right."

Perhaps the most revealing point in the *Fulton* oral argument arose in Justice Barrett's questioning of Jeffrey

Fischer, representing a gay foster care group. Justice Barrett began the question with the following stipulation: "I think we would agree that there's really not any circumstance we can think of in which racial discrimination would be permitted as a religious exemption." Justice Barrett then asked Fischer: "Can you think of any example in which saying, as, you know, CSS has done here, that they, you know, will not certify same-sex couples, that—where an objection to same-sex marriage would justify an exemption? Or is it like racial discrimination?"

Justice Barrett's stipulation—that we can all "agree that there's really not any circumstance we can think of in which racial discrimination would be permitted as a religious exemption"—highlights the changes to our system wrought by the canonization of *Brown*. Why could she assert so confidently that we can all agree that there is not a single possible situation in which private racial discrimination would not be part of the guarantee of the free exercise of religion?

Here, it is important to note that this consensus does not come from a single case dealing with religious liberty and racial discrimination. In fact, there is only one major case on that subject and that case applied to the particular context of higher education and tax exemptions.[55] So, if not from a particular case, where does this consensus come from?

The consensus comes from the system that the canonization of *Brown* created. To participate in this system, we must agree that, regardless of the Constitution's original purpose or meaning on a particular subject, we must treat private racial discrimination as a constitutional evil and racial diversity as a constitutional good. Judges and scholars may identify as originalists and living constitutionalists. But above all else, they are antiracists.

III. THE WAY OUT

This *Provocations* essay has demonstrated that the best way to understand Ibram X. Kendi's proposed antiracist constitutional amendment is not as an act of rebellion, working against the system, but rather as an extension of our current order, working within the civil rights regime. Understood in this light, Kendi and his fellow critical race theorists are not civil rights revolutionaries but civil rights managers. This is a significant distinction for how we think about the current regime. It suggests that we should spend less time focusing on the scandal of "wokeness" and critical race theory and more time focusing on how we got here in the first place. With a better understanding of how we got here, we can develop a better understanding of how our antiracist order works. This will pay off dividends, especially in fighting affirmative action and identity politics.

For decades conservatives have been arguing that anti-discrimination law will put an end to racial preferences. Conservatives have erred in predicting affirmative action's demise because they misunderstand the nature of the civil rights regime. Indeed, they ignore how anti-discrimination law grew in tandem with affirmative action practices. As explained in this essay, anti-discrimination law and affirmative action are part of the same system—according to which racial discrimination is our greatest evil and diversity is our greatest good. In this system, racial discrimination can never be permitted unless it is used to promote diversity, in which case racial discrimination is not only permitted but required.

A successful attack on affirmative action will therefore require a broader challenge to the antiracist constitutional order. This will requires depathologizing race as a constitutional matter. While this does not entail or warrant neglecting the moral and intellectual problems that inhere in racist ideologies, it does require opening up space to dissent on racial matters. We must be free to debate

Brown and the broader civil rights revolution, including their constitutional, political, and sociological merits. In a healthy constitutional system, there can be no *Brown* litmus test.

This means that the two moral axioms arising from the canonization of *Brown*—that privately expressed racial discrimination is uniquely evil and racial diversity is uniquely good—must be subject to examination. We must be free to explore when private discrimination is protected as a constitutional right. The specter of racism cannot hang over structural arguments for federalism and the state action doctrine and individual liberty arguments for the freedom of association and free exercise of religion. Likewise, we must be free to probe when diversity is not a source of strength but of weakness.

H. L. Mencken once described Puritanism as driven by "the haunting fear that someone, somewhere, may be happy." The canonization of *Brown* has brought a puritanical character to our constitutional system. Only we are driven not by the Puritans' fear of pleasure but by the antiracists' fear of discrimination. And we are motivated not by the glory of God but by the glory of diversity.

Decanonizing *Brown* means driving out this puritanical way of thinking about race. If this means there will be some discrimination and lack of diversity in some corners of American life, so be it. We cannot overhaul our entire order because of the haunting fear that someone, somewhere, may be a racist.

ABOUT THE AUTHOR

Jesse Merriam is a Washington Fellow at the Claremont Institute's Center for the American Way of Life and an associate professor of government at Patrick Henry College in Purcellville, Virginia. Merriam has published over a dozen articles in peer-reviewed and law-review journals, and is a frequent contributor to Law & Liberty. His writing focuses on constitutional theory, civil rights law, and legal conservatism. He holds an MA in philosophy and a PhD in political science from Johns Hopkins University, and a JD from George Washington University Law School.

ENDNOTES

1. Ibram X. Kendi, "Pass an Anti-Racist Constitutional Amendment," *Politico*, accessed June 7, 2023, https://www.politico.com/interactives/2019/how-to-fix-politics-in-america/inequality/pass-an-anti-racist-constitutional-amendment/.

2. Much of the scholarship on canonization stems from J. M. Balkin and Sanford Levinson, "The Canons of Constitutional Law," *Harvard Law Review* 111, no. 4 (1998): 963.

3. In Balkin and Levinson's words, "the standard constitutional law course might well be understood as organized around the ritual justification and demonization of specific canonical [and anti-canonical] cases." Indeed, "one sometimes feels that all of modern constitutional theory is driven by a desire to justify (or condemn) five cases (and we all know which ones they are)."

4. As Balkin and Levinson write, "the canon is like a set of doctrinal dots that any theory of constitutional law must connect," so that the canon constitutes the baseline for "construct[ing] and test[ing] relevant theories of constitutional law and constitutional adjudication."

5. For example, even originalists like Randy Barnett and Josh Blackman concede that "constitutional law is actually practiced—and doctrine developed—by hewing to the canonical cases, while avoiding those in the 'anti-canon.'" For this reason, Barnett and Blackman arrange their constitutional law casebook according to the canon and anti-canon so as to "provide[] the basic vocabulary of constitutional law." Randy Barnett, "Teaching the Canon and the Anti-Canon of Constitutional Law," *Washington Post*, October 23, 2021, https://www.washingtonpost.com/news/volokh-conspiracy/wp/2017/09/09/teaching-the-canon-and-the-anti-canon-of-constitutional-law/.

6. Jerry Goldman, *Is There A Canon of Constitutional Law?* (Boston, MA: Department of Political Science, Northeastern University, 1992) is the most empirically oriented work on canonization. That work reviewed twelve leading constitutional law casebooks, amounting to a total of 552 different principal Supreme Court cases, to determine which cases appeared most frequently. Goldman found that only *Brown*, *Griswold*, and *Roe* were common to all twelve books. Given that *Roe* has been overruled and that, as a result, *Griswold* is now of dubious validity, it follows from Goldman's empirical analysis that *Brown* is the core canonical case.

7. For example, in their 1998 Harvard Law Review article, Balkin and Levison proclaimed that "the classic example of a 'must explain' case, of course, is *Brown v. Board of Education*" (Balkin and Levinson, 1018). Two years later, in an important article on the role conservatives played in canonizing the *Brown* decision, a subject that will be analyzed later in this essay, Brad Snyder observed that "*Brown v. Board of Education* is the sacred cow of American constitutional law." See Brad Snyder, "How the Conservatives Canonized Brown v. Board of Education," *Rutgers Law Review* 52, no. 383, October 8, 2009, https://ssrn.com/abstract=1485466. In fact, Snyder wrote, "*Brown's* place in the upper canon is more secure than any other Supreme Court precedent," and "not even *Marbury v. Madison* is universally endorsed the way *Brown* is." Jamal Greene, a Columbia Law professor and one of the leading scholars studying canonization, observed that *Brown* "is the classic example" of a canonical decision "whose correctness participants in constitutional argument must always assume." See Jamal Greene, "The Anticanon," *Harvard Law Review* 125, no. 2 (2011): 380–475.

8. Michael C. Dorf, "Stare Decisis and Originalism," *Dorf on Law*, October 23, 2015, http://www.dorfonlaw.org/2015/10/stare-decisis-and-originalism.html.

9. The Garland Fund was created in 1922 after young Charles Garland inherited nearly $1 million (worth roughly $17 million in today's dollars) from his deceased father, who was at the time one of the nation's wealthiest bankers. As a devout communist, Charles initially decided to reject the inheritance. But he was later convinced by Roger Baldwin (who had just

founded the American Civil Liberties Union) to accept the inheritance and support left-wing causes with the money.

10. For example, Lisa M. Stulberg and Anthony S. Chen ("The Origins of Race-Conscious Affirmative Action in Undergraduate Admissions," *Sociology of Education* 87, no. 1 [November 2013]: 36–52) found that between 1954 (the year *Brown* was decided) and 1964 (the year the civil rights legislation was passed into law), ten private and public institutions formally adopted affirmative action programs (Harvard, Dartmouth, Columbia, Penn, Brown, Cornell, UCLA, Michigan, Swarthmore, and Wesleyan). Stulberg and Chen further found that many of these schools explicitly linked the creation of their affirmative action programs to *Brown* and the civil rights movement.

11. Anthony S. Chen and Lisa M. Stulberg, "Before Bakke: The Hidden History of the Diversity Rationale," *University of Chicago Law Review Online*, October 30, 2020, https://lawreviewblog.uchicago.edu/2020/10/30/aa-chen-stulberg/.

12. *Porcelli v. Titus*, 302 F. Supp. 726 (D.N.J. 1969).

13. Ibid., 732.

14. Ibid., 732.

15. Ibid., 736.

16. *Porcelli v. Titus*, 431 F.2d 1254, 1257-58 (3d Cir. 1970).

17. See *Kemp v. Beasley*, 352 F.2d 14 (8th Cir. 1965); *Bradley v. Richmond School Board*, 345 F.2d 310 (4th Cir. 1965).

18. *Singleton v. Jackson Municipal Separate School District I*, 348 F.2d 729 (5th Cir. 1965); *Singleton v. Jackson Municipal Separate School District II*, 355 F.2d 865 (5th Cir. 1966); *U.S. v. Jefferson County Board of Education*, 372 F.2d 836 (5th Cir. 1966).

19. 380 F.2d 385 (5th Cir. 1967).

20. On *National Review*'s role in constructing constitutional conservatism, see Ken I. Kersch, "Ecumenicalism Through Constitutionalism: The Discursive Development of Constitutional Conservatism in *National Review*, 1955-1980," *Studies in American Political Development* 25 (spring 2011): 86–116.

21. See Frank Meyer, "Principles and Heresies," *National Review*, June 6, 1959 (referring to Brown as a "notorious" example of "sociological generalization and majoritarian expediency"); Frank Meyer, "The Court Challenges the Congress," *National Review*, March 24, 1964 (claiming that *Brown* "boldly usurped the legislative powers reserved by the Constitution to the Congress and the legislatures of the several states and promulgated a dictate affecting the lives of individual citizens, the sovereignty of the states, and the prerogatives of the Congress").

22. See James Burnham, "Why Not Investigate the Court?" *National Review*, July 20, 1957 (explaining why *Brown* is an illegitimate decision that has worsened American race relations and that warrants a congressional investigation of the Court's conduct).

23. See Willmoore Kendall, "Light on an American Dilemma," *National Review*, November 5, 1960 (speculating, in a review of a book on biology and race, that integration of cities and schools might destroy America).

24. See Richard Weaver, "Integration Is Communization," *National Review*, July 13, 1957 (explaining how cases like *Brown* and *Shelley* operate "as a crowbar to pry loose rights over private property").

25. For example, in a March 11, 1961 article, "Footnote to Brown v. Board of Education," Buckley condemned "coercive integrationists" as being either ignorant about or malicious toward the South. In an October 23, 1962 article, "The Mess in Mississippi—An Afterword," Buckley defended Southern resistance against *Brown*, which he characterized as an instance of the Supreme Court "decid[ing] to bestow on their subjects a brand-new natural right." In a May 21, 1963 article, "Birmingham and After," Buckley again defended Southern resistance, on the ground that *Brown* created a constitutional order "utterly unrelated to the Constitution the South grew up swearing allegiance to."

26. Consider the following sample to get a flavor of the views expressed in these *National Review* editorials. A September 21, 1957 editorial proclaimed that race relations would be better served by the *Plessy* "separate but equal" doctrine. "The Court Views Its Handiwork," *National Review*, Sep-

tember 21, 1957. An October 25, 1958 editorial expressed concern that enforcing *Brown* would lead to increased anti-Semitism, because "organized Jewish groups have noisily egged on the court, and aggressively called for immediate implementation of its [desegregation] decisions." "The Court Reaps Its Whirlwind," *National Review*, October 25, 1958. A few weeks later, a *National Review* editorial accused the NAACP, Department of Justice, and federal courts of engaging in "active collusion" against the South. "The Integration Siege," *National Review*, November 15, 1958. A January 17, 1959 editorial claimed that "Negroes will suffer the most" as a result of *Brown* because in an integrated society "the Negro may find that he has been effectively deracinated." "Solution for the South?" *National Review*, January 17, 1959. An August 15, 1959 editorial expressed concern that *Brown* would lead to efforts to ban racial discrimination in private education. "The Week," *National Review*, August 15, 1959. A September 12, 1959 editorial explained how courts had begun the process of banning private discrimination and how "before *Brown v. Board of Education* these idiocies would have been laughable." "The Week," *National Review*, September 12, 1959. A January 30, 1960 editorial critiqued the Republican Party for accepting *Brown* while asserting states' rights, a position that is sufficiently conflicting "to confound intellectually-minded folk." "The Week," *National Review*, January 30, 1960. A March 26, 1960 editorial claimed that *Brown* represents the "sweep[ing] [of] American institutions under the carpet." "The Week," *National Review*, March 26, 1960. A December 2, 1961 editorial asserted that the NAACP's resistance to "white flight" might lead to totalitarianism, for white flight is simply a product of "a continuing, deeply rooted community feeling against a total commingling of the races—a feeling that cannot be artificially eradicated by court decree, at least in a society that does not engage in totalitarian methods." "Earl Warren Proposes...," *National Review*, December 2, 1961. Similarly, an April 10, 1962 editorial characterized *Brown* as "the prime symbol of the drive toward a centralized, despotic mass state that has been proceeding under the direction of a united front of the federal executive and judiciary." See "Toward the Total State," *National Review*, April 10, 1962. A November 11, 1962 response to "To the Editor" letters summarized the *National Review* position on *Brown*: "For seven years National Review has fought for states' rights, continuing to disapprove, *inter alia*, of *Brown v. Board of Education*." See "To the Editor," *National Review*, November 11, 1962.

27. In Hand's view, *Brown* could be justified as a constitutional decision only if "racial equality [is] a value that must prevail against any conflicting interests." Since Judge Hand could find no such principle in the Constitution itself or in the court's precedents, Judge Hand concluded that *Brown* was an illegitimate decision. This presentation was later assembled into a book, *The Bill of Rights* (1958).

28. Wechsler was a professor at Columbia Law, a coauthor of the most important casebook on federal courts, and the leader of the Legal Process School of legal interpretation.

29. Hannah Arendt, "Reflections on Little Rock," *Dissent Magazine*, Winter 1959, https://www.dissentmagazine.org/article/reflections-on-little-rock.

30. In Arendt's words, "without discrimination of some sort, society would simply cease to exist and very important possibilities of free association and group formation would disappear." Arendt argued that private discrimination is particularly important in racially heterogeneous societies: "because of the extraordinary heterogeneity of [the American] population, social conformism [as expressed in anti-discrimination laws] tends to become an absolute and a substitute for national homogeneity."

31. Ken I. Kersch, "The Alternative Tradition of Conservative Constitutional Theory," in *Conservatives and the Constitution: Imagining Constitutional Restoration in the Heyday of American Liberalism* (New York: Cambridge University Press, 2019), 27–102.

32. Brad Snyder, "How the Conservatives Canonized Brown v. Board of Education," *Rutgers Law Review* 52, no. 383, October 8, 2009, https://ssrn.com/abstract=1485466.

33. See William F. Buckley, "On the Right," *National Review*, January 5, 1973 (arguing that he still believes *Brown* was decided incorrectly, but he is starting to see that compulsory desegregation may make the South more congenial to the North, and this may facilitate a coalition between Southern conservatives and Northern Republicans); James Kilpatrick,

"This Much, at Least: The Court," *National Review*, September 28, 1973 (claiming that Brown "was clearly a monstrosity; but the opinion served to smash a rotten barrier").

34. Jack Chatfield, "A Story from the Border," *National Review*, August 6, 1976 (providing a positive review of Richard Kluger's recently published book, *Simple Justice*, and agreeing with Kluger that *Brown* was right both morally and legally).

35. Bork's *New Republic* article attacked the civil rights bill on constitutional and policy grounds, noting that the "proponents of the legislation" have "ignore[d] the fact that [applying anti-discrimination law to private business] means a loss in a vital area of personal liberty." In Bork's view, the underlying logic of the civil rights legislation—i.e., the logic that "I am justified in having the state coerce you into more righteous paths"—represented "a principle of unsurpassed ugliness."

36. Ethan Bronner, *Battle for Justice: How the Bork Nomination Shook America* (New York: W. W. Norton, 1989).

37. As Richard Posner observed in 1990, "no constitutional theory that implies that *Brown v. Board of Education*... was decided incorrectly will receive a fair hearing nowadays." See Richard A. Posner, "Bork and Beethoven," *Stanford Law Review* 42, no. 6 (1990): 1374. Likewise, Cass Sunstein noted in 1993 that "an approach to constitutional interpretation is unacceptable if it entails the incorrectness of *Brown v. Board of Education*." See Cass R. Sunstein, "In Defense of Liberal Education," *Journal of Legal Education* 43, no. 1 (1993): 26.

38. See Thomas Sowell, "Brown Out," *National Review*, December 12, 2006; Thomas Sowell, "One of the Best Schools for Black Students Was Ruined by Good Intentions," *National Review*, October 5, 2016.

39. For example, one of these articles, by Edward Blum and Roger Clegg, proclaimed that "No other case in modern history has had such a positive effect on our society." See Edward Blum and Roger Clegg, "A Long Way From '54," *National Review*, May 17, 2004. Another one of these articles, by Peter Kirsanow, explained why *Brown* should be commemorated for articulating the American notion of justice. See Peter Kirsanow, "The Glass Is Half Full," *National Review*, May 25, 2004.

40. Ronald D. Rotunda ,"There's No Future in the Past of Campaign Finance," *National Review* (June 28, 2006).

41. Ramesh Ponnuru, "Liberals v. Umpres," *National Review* (July 1, 2010).

42. Maggie Gallagher, "What I Want GOP Candidates to Say about Marriage," *National Review* (June 26, 2015).

43. Michael W. McConnell, Originalism and the Desegregation Decisions, 81 Va. L. Rev. 947 (1995). Raoul Berger, who had written an entire book in 1977 on why an originalist understanding of the Fourteenth Amendment did not warrant the *Brown* decision, assailed McConnell's article for hijacking into an originalist interpretation historical evidence from nearly ten years after the Fourteenth Amendment was debated and ratified. See Raoul Berger, "The 'Original Intent'—As Perceived by Michael McConnell," 91 *Nw. U.L. Rev.* 242 (1996). But Berger's criticism was generally ignored, as it was clear that, in a post-Bork political environment, originalism had to accommodate *Brown* if it was going to survive.

44. We see this in how many Republican-nominated Supreme Court justices have cited the McConnell article to support the notion that the *Brown* decision is consistent with the original public meaning of the Fourteenth Amendment. Similarly, in 2005 Ed Whelan wrote a series of *National Review* articles using the McConnell argument as evidence of how *Brown* is consistent with originalism. See Ed Whelan, "Brown and Originalism," *National Review*, May 11, 2005; Ed Whelan, "Playing Make-Believe," *National Review*, May 12, 2005; Ed Whelan, "An Unoriginal Argument," *National Review*, May 19, 2005; Ed Whelan, "A Postscript on Brown and Originalism," *National Review*, May 23, 2005.

45. This is evident in how, following the McConnell article, many of the leading *National Review* writers began revising the publication's history to make it appear to have been consistent in supporting *Brown*. For example, in a 2005 article, Deroy Murdock proclaimed that *Brown* and other civil rights achievements are actually conservative victories. See Deroy Murdock, "Grand Old Party," *National Review*, February 18, 2005. Over the last several years, Kevin Williamson has written several articles on how the Republican Party is responsible for *Brown* and the resulting civil rights movement. In one

such article, Williamson explained how Senator Goldwater (despite voting against the Civil Rights Act of 1964) favored *Brown*, which Williamson described as "one of the great landmarks of American history." See Kevin Williamson, "Desegregation, before Brown," *National Review*, April 29, 2013. In another article, Williamson argued that President Eisenhower is a great conservative who "finished some of Lincoln's work, especially regarding access to education and economic opportunity" by desegregating "those schools and institutions over which he had direct federal power as president more than a year before Brown v. Board of Education was decided." See Kevin Williamson, "Why Like Ike—Conservatives Got Eisenhower Wrong the First Time Around," *National Review*, September 2, 2013. Williamson comes very close to outright lying in another article on *Brown*, where he claims that "many conservatives at the time [of *Brown*]... shared the views of Barry Goldwater, who was himself an advocate of desegregation." Even more audaciously, Williamson contends that Goldwater's desegregation position "was the view of most of the editors of *National Review* at the time" and how, between 1955 and the mid-1960s, the publication had "relatively little ... to say about" the decision. See Kevin Williamson, "Brown-ian Motion," *National Review*, May 14, 2014. Both of these claims are inaccurate. As mentioned above, between 1955 (when *National Review* was formed) and 1968, the publication featured over thirty-five articles on the *Brown* decision, and all of these treated the decision negatively. Many of these articles were written by the *National Review* editors, including several by the publication's founder, William F. Buckley.

46. This weaponization generally falls into four categories. One category of weaponization has been in the realm of abortion law. Indeed, *National Review* has published several articles celebrating how the *Brown* Court overruled *Plessy*, and arguing on this basis that the court would similarly be justified in overruling *Roe* and the cases it produced. Another area of weaponization has been in the context of gay rights. As the gay rights movement gained momentum in the early twenty-first century, *National Review* published several articles claiming that gay rights advocates, by using cases like *Brown* and *Loving* to advance their cause in terms of anti-discrimination and family law, were undermining the Judeo-Chris-

tian commitments underlying the civil rights movement. A third use has been in opposing affirmative action and identity politics as a whole. After conservatives began embracing *Brown*, they sought to reconstruct it as a decision about the constitutional impropriety of race-based legislation and identity politics. A fourth category has involved weaponization of *Brown* in disputes over voucher programs and related school-choice issues. In 2002 alone, the year the Supreme Court heard *Zelman v. Simmons-Harris* (2002)—a case involving whether a Cleveland K-12 voucher program violated the Establishment Clause by funding religiously affiliated private schools—there were five *National Review* articles celebrating *Brown* and using it as a weapon to defend voucher programs. Jay P. Greene, "The New Brown," *National Review*, February 21, 2002; Richard W. Garnett, "Choice Wins," *National Review*, June 27, 2002; Ted Cruz, "This One's for the Children," *National Review*, June 28, 2002; John J. Miller, "What's Next for School Choice?" *National Review*, June 28, 2002; John J. Miller, "School Choice, Not an Echo," *National Review*, June 29, 2002.

47. Indeed, here is how he completed his brief to the Supreme Court:

> Many of the themes in this case reflect those raised 47 years ago in *Brown v. Board of Education*. There, children were forced to travel past good neighborhood schools to attend inferior schools because the children happened to be black; today, many poor children are forced to travel past good schools to attend inferior schools because the schools happen to be private. In the quest to fulfill the promise of equal educational opportunity, we must enlist every resource at our disposal. The Cleveland Pilot Scholarship Program was not designed to test the boundaries of constitutional law, but to fit safely within them. We respectfully ask this honorable Court to affirm that it does.

Incidentally, these themes were picked up in Justice Thomas's concurring opinion. Justice Thomas (who was Bolick's mentor at the EEOC and is the godfather to Bolick's son) began his concurring opinion in *Zelman* by citing *Brown* and suggesting that the Cleveland public school system amounts to a betrayal of *Brown*'s promise to black children.

48. In 2019, the *Washington Post* counted thirteen unarmed black men who were killed by police officers. See "Fatal Force: Police Shootings Database," *Washington Post*, January 22, 2020, https://www.washingtonpost.com/graphics/investigations/police-shootings-database/. By comparison, about sixty Americans die each year from hornet, wasp, and bee stings, and about thirty Americans die each year from lightning strikes. See "*QuickStats*: Number of Deaths from Hornet, Wasp, and Bee Stings, Among Females and Males—National Vital Statistics System, United States, 2000–2017," *Morbidity and Mortality Weekly Report*, CDC, July 26, 2019, https://www.cdc.gov/mmwr/volumes/68/wr/mm6829a5.htm; "U.S. Lightning Strike Deaths," Natural Disasters and Severe Weather, CDC, accessed June 7, 2023, https://www.cdc.gov/disasters/lightning/victimdata/infographic.html#:~:text=On%20average%2C%2028%20people%20in,reported%20from%202006%20through%202021.

49. *Federal Trade Commission v Raymond Bros.-Clark Co.*, 263 U.S. 565, 573 (1924).

50. *McElhenney Co. v. Western Auto Supply Co.*, 269 F.2d 332, 337 (4th Cir. 1959).

51. For example, the words "race" and "gay" appeared at almost the same rate ("race" appeared twenty-seven times and "gay" appeared twenty-eight times). In addition, the terms "African-American" and "black" were each used six times, and "interracial marriage" and the "Ku Klux Klan" were each discussed four times.

52. "ACLU-VA & Partners Investigate All Communication between the Hanover County School Board and Alliance Defending Freedom," ACLU Virginia, March 11, 2022, https://www.acluva.org/en/press-releases/aclu-va-partners-investigate-all-communication-between-hanover-county-school-board.

53. "ACLU Has Filed 400 Legal Actions against Trump Administration," ACLU, August 17, 2020, https://www.aclu.org/press-releases/aclu-has-filed-400-legal-actions-against-trump-administration.

54. The word "interracial" was used thirteen times, as the justices kept coming back to the question of whether, if religious liberty meant that CSS could deny service to same-same cou-

ples, some other hypothetical group would then have the right to deny service for interracial couples.

55. The *Bob Jones* decision is itself revealing of the principle I have been developing here. In *Bob Jones v. U.S.* (1983), a conservative Christian college lost its tax-exempt status because it opposed interracial marriage. Although the Supreme Court accepted that the college's religious exercise was "substantially burdened" by this penalty, in that the college opposed interracial marriage on biblical grounds and losing its tax-exempt status would essentially require the college to violate its religious commitments, the Supreme Court held that the Free Exercise Clause permitted the penalty, because "*Brown v. Board of Education* establishes beyond doubt this Court's view that racial discrimination in education violates a most fundamental national public policy." In other words, religious liberty had to be limited because of the constitutional order created by *Brown*.

Made in the USA
Middletown, DE
22 September 2025